AU& I:
A Guide to
Autism Inclusion

ABENA ARTHUR

Copyright © 2023 Constance R.M. Turrentine

All rights reserved.

ISBN:
9798377267003

DEDICATION

Dedicating this book to the memory of my mother as a testament to her unwavering passion for helping those in need. She was a selfless human being who touched the lives of many. Her devotion to serving the homeless inspired me to pursue a career in teaching. My mother believed in me and encouraged me to chase my dreams, even when I was uncertain. Her tragic death in 2015, was a loss not only to her family but also to the countless individuals she had helped throughout her life.

Her legacy continues to shape my scope as a teacher, and her life serves as a constant reminder of the power of compassion, kindness, and dedication. I am honored to dedicate this book to her memory and strive to be a voice for the voiceless—advocating for those who are differently abled. I hope to empower individuals with autism to reach their full potential and live fulfilling lives. May my mothers spirit live on through this body of work and inspire future generations.

"You'll never be a teacher….if you don't get started." Constance Peters

—Thank you Lady. I am YOUR Legacy. I will continue to lead with love.

CONTENTS

Chapter1: Importance of Independent Work Skills
Chapter 2:Understanding Autism
Chapter 3:Developing Awareness and Self Advocacy
Chapter 4: Encouraging Self Determination and Positive Behaviors
Chapter 5: Building Positive Relationships
Chapter 6: Improving Engagement and Inclusion
Chapter 7: Building Self-Esteem
Chapter 8: Application of Supportive Techniques
Chapter 9: Ways to Get Started
Chapter 10: Community Inclusion
ABOUT THE AUTHOR

ACKNOWLEDGMENTS

As parents, educator, caregivers, or caring community members, it is our goal to empower our young adults regardless of a diagnosis to become functioning members of their communities. To achieve this, it is essential to focus on developing essential life skills such as independent work skills. Using these practical strategies and techniques can help young adults with autism improve their independence and become more engaged in every aspect of their lives.

Autism, also known as Autism Spectrum Disorder (ASD), is a neurodevelopmental disorder that affects communication, social interaction, and behavior. Individuals with challenging cognitive development may also experience difficulties with independent work skills due to learning disabilities, intellectual disabilities, or other developmental delays.

Chapter 1: The Importance of Independent Work Skills

It is important to understand the unique needs and challenges faced by the individual to effectively support their development. These individuals may struggle with executive functioning skills, social skills, and sensory processing, which can impact their ability to complete tasks independently.

Awareness and self-advocacy are critical skills to becoming more successful, independent members of society. Awareness involves being aware of one's own abilities, strengths, and weaknesses, as well as the environment and situations they are in. Self-advocacy involves speaking up for oneself, expressing one's needs and opinions, and making informed decisions. That can be hard at times especially if the person has a speech delay or doesn't have the tools to communicate appropriately.

To improve awareness, it is recommended to engage young adults in various activities and experiences that promote self-reflection and self-awareness. These activities could include journaling using pictures or object, creating digital prompt boards, visual goal-setting with reinforcers, and adapted self-assessments which can be pictorial and / or written choices that represent a set of preferences.

To promote self-advocacy, it is important to provide opportunities for young adults to practice speaking up for themselves in safe and supportive environments. This can be done through role-playing activities, assertiveness training, and encouraging them to ask for what they need. Communication can improve the total well being of the person in care and can significantly impact they way they are relieved as well as how they see themselves in their environment.

Engagement refers to the level of involvement and interest in a particular activity or environment. Its one thing to do what's asked. Its another to actually be apart. Inclusion refers to the sense of belonging and being valued as a member of a group or community. If the community or area in which a person with autism is not reflected of the things that interests or appeals to that person, why would they participate. If we experience that we remove ourselves from that environment and seek comforts that support us. Improving engagement and inclusion can help young adults with autism feel more connected and valued in their communities. Feelings matter

Independent work skills are crucial for differentiating ability individuals as it leads them to desire more fulfilling and productive lives. These skills involve the ability to complete tasks, make decisions, and manage time and resources effectively. Independent work skills enable more self-sufficiency, confidence, and engagement– sometime being more open to try new things

> Examples of independent work skills include:
> - Cooking and meal preparation
> - Cleaning and household chores
> - Budgeting and money management
> - Time management and scheduling
> - Problem-solving and decision-making
> - Self-care and personal hygiene

Having strong independent work skills can improve their overall quality of life, and increase their chances of success in work, school, and relationships. The impact of letting go to let them try produces amazing outcomes as they are not hindered by preconceived shortcoming often projected by the fears of others onto them. Because more people around there are their to support, some support can lend itself to being an obstacle that adds to self-doubt, anxiety and learned helplessness. These can be difficult behaviors to replace if someone who cares for them is unable to allow their responses to change. You'd be surprised how non-verbal, even emotional cues from those around them can make a difference in their pursuit for independence.

Differently abled people are not their behaviors rather are responding to the signals in their environment often through their emotions. Patterns of positive outcome will lead to repeat behavior just as negative outcome results in negative response. By structuring positive outcomes while encouraging positive feedback builds the confidence to work toward getting better at new skills over time. Let's face it, no one lives forever. Creating dependence does not forest growth. It implies that attempt to do things should "only" happen during " certain " conditions, which isn't ideal for progress. It's important to expand beyond conditioning and create chances for critical thinking. After all, this is a skill all adults need to navigate.

Objectives of the Book

The objective of this book is to provide practical strategies and techniques to help young adults with autism to improve their independent work skills and celebrate being differently- abled to

- Increase awareness and self-advocacy skills
- Encourage self-determination and positive behaviors
- Improve engagement and inclusion in their communities

- Build self-esteem and confidence in their abilities
- Provide practical examples and real-life scenarios to implement these strategies in real-time.

The most inclusive techniques offer the tools and support they need to achieve their goals and become successful and as independent as possible.

It is recommended to provide opportunities for activities and experiences that they find relevant and enjoyable. Being made to do what they cant relate to will only create a negative experience. This could include community service projects, hobbies, and interests. Enrichment experiences can give them a change to explore what their true interest is. Be prepared to gage their feeling about things that they do such as " Did you like that?" or " Do you want to do that again?". What a great time to encourage communication to reinforce the purpose and power of their words.

Chapter 2: Understanding Autism

What is Autism?

Autism Spectrum Disorder (ASD) is a neurodevelopmental disorder that affects communication, social interaction, and behavior. It is a spectrum disorder, meaning that the symptoms and severity can vary greatly from person to person. Individuals with challenging cognitive development may also experience difficulties with learning and intellectual development.

Individuals may experience a range of symptoms, including:

- Communication difficulties, including delayed speech and language development
- Social challenges, such as difficulty making friends and interacting with others
- Repetitive behaviors and routines
- Sensory sensitivities, such as an aversion to certain textures or sounds
- Executive functioning difficulties, including organization, planning, and decision-making

The characteristics of their abilities can be challenging but with consistency and clear expectations development of learn skill may be gradual but ultimately improve independent work skills. Stay the course.

Compromising and changing expectations only leads to delays in understanding what is being asked as its too much to process and becomes overwhelming to understand.

Calling a person's name or attention to something over and over can be less helpful and distracting because like asking the person to buffer and start over and over instead of completing what is asked from start to finish. This is because they may have difficulties with executive functioning skills which can make it challenging to plan and complete tasks, while sensory sensitivities may make certain household chores difficult to perform.

The sensory aspect is so important as we are able to possess the information we receive in our environment such as sound, temperatures and other things that people with autism often become triggered by. Understanding these challenges and the unique needs of each individual is essential to effectively support their development and improve their independent work skills.

Self-determination refers to the ability to make choices and decisions for oneself, with a sense of control over one's own life. Giving models of set expectations can influence positive behaviors and lead to behaviors that are socially acceptable, productive, and respectful. Encouraging self-determination and positive behaviors can help young adults with autism become more confident, independent, and engaged in everything they do.

To teach self-determination, it is important to provide opportunities to do so within a supportive and safe environment. This can be done through goal-setting activities, decision-making exercises, and providing them with choices whenever possible.

It is recommended to use positive reinforcement techniques, such as praising and rewarding good behavior. It is also important to provide clear and consistent rules and consequences, and to model positive behaviors. Although edibles and offering rewards such as screen time on a electronic may work, these should be faded over time to prevent fixation and lead to the development of new behaviors.

Replacing items and gaining more on target behavior for smaller or more internally motivated reinforces will help gain the success for the individual. Remember, it takes time. Behavior can get worst before they get better. That is why it is important to stay consistent. Eventually, there will a point where the individual will seek to do the requested task and be more engaged.

It is also recommended to use evidence-based strategies, such as structured teaching, visual supports, and positive reinforcement. With the right support and guidance, these individuals have the potential to develop strong skills, desensitize triggers that lead to negative responses and replace them with positive lead fulfilling, successful lives.

Chapter 3: Developing Awareness and Self Advocacy

Awareness and self-advocacy are essential skills. Being aware of one's own needs and preferences, as well as having the ability to communicate these needs to others, can greatly improve their quality of life. Awareness and self-advocacy also empower individuals to take control of their own lives, making decisions and pursuing opportunities that align with their values and goals.

Self-advocacy is particularly important in situations where individuals may not have a caregiver or support system to advocate on their behalf. By speaking up for themselves and making their needs known, individuals can ensure that their voices are heard and that their rights are respected.

Strategies for Improving Awareness

Self-Reflection: Encourage individuals to take time to reflect on their thoughts, feelings, and needs. This can be done through journaling, meditation, or simply taking a few moments to focus inward. Seeing yourself in your environment is important motivator to take part in it.

Communication Skills Training: Teach individuals how to effectively communicate their needs and wants to others. This can include learning how to use clear and concise language, making eye contact, and expressing emotions appropriately. Behavior is often the most overlooked communication tool most persons with autism has access too. Help them to strengthen their voice by validating their frustration through offering an opportunity to express it appropriately. It makes a world of a difference when they are able to voice how they feel using their personal mode of communication. Don't Just talk at them allow pauses to wait on small responses, gestures, guiding to areas to open up for greater discussion or gauging facial expression.

Social Skills Training: Encourage individuals to engage in social activities and interactions. This can help them gain a better understanding of their own preferences, as well as learn how to navigate social situations. It's one thing to understand the meaning if self control but it can impact their lives being around peers who are modeling on task behaviors. It helps to start small with an engagement lasting for minutes at a time. Increasing the time can improve tolerance of this new experience. It is helpful to talk about what will happen before it happens. It matters. Providing a snapshot of what is expected and who is coming into their space helps to decrease anxiety and often allows for a positive experience. It's get tough when you are trying to understand your own behavior let alone someone else's. Once that fear factor goes away so does barriers to social interactions. Before you know it, tolerance for others can broaden to becoming comfortable with groups of people around them and dare I say— encourage making friends or other that are permitted to comfortably frequent their personal space.

Role-Playing: Encourage individuals to practice advocating for themselves in role-playing scenarios. This can help them build confidence and feel more comfortable speaking up in real-life situations. Modeling, both video and in person, is an effective way of communicating what is expected of your differently-abled individual. It takes time to get a solid understanding of knowing what to do next. It is helpful especially when you want to encourage your person to move to start on an activity and follow through to complete the activity. Understanding what first, next or last requires repeated examples. At times you can show them what the final step is and build til all the steps are completed to make the activity achievable.

Techniques for Self Advocacy Training

1. Empowerment Workshops: Attend workshops or training sessions that focus on empowering individuals to speak up for themselves and assert their rights.
2.
3. Support Groups: Join a support group where individuals can connect with others who share similar experiences and learn from one another. Surf the web there are plenty to research.
4.

5.   Mentorship Programs: Participate in mentorship programs that pair individuals with experienced self-advocates who can offer guidance and support.
6.
7.   Practice, Practice, Practice: Encourage individuals to practice advocating for themselves in real-life situations. The more they do it, the more confident and comfortable they will become. Remember to always encourage attempts toward independence despite your own personal fears or behavioral outburst. As with any other person, success has its balance of trial and error, wins and losses. Pick your battles but never be afraid to try and as for support when possible

Chapter 4: Encouraging Self Determination and Positive Behaviors

Sometimes there are behaviors that have been developed out of an attempt to self soothe. Self calming can vary amongst individuals, but you know your person well enough to identify what he or she does or needs to return to a peaceful state. That is definitely a positive sign that regulating one's behavior is a goal and they may be seeking the only resources they have discovered for themselves. Protection and safety is an overlooked priority and should be noted and celebrated for making an effort to uphold it – regardless of what it looks like to others.

Self-determination refers to the ability to make choices and decisions that are in line with one's own values, goals, and desires. This can include decisions related to one's education, employment, housing, personal relationships and can include safety.

Self-determination is an important aspect of an individual's overall well-being and sense of autonomy. By making decisions that are in line with their own values and goals, individuals are more likely to feel fulfilled and satisfied with their lives. Often people insert their values or even their fears and it can add to the power struggle. It's important to observe what the behavior is "saying" and encourage more appropriate communication in its place.

Importance of Positive Behaviors

Positive behaviors are crucial for individuals with developmental disabilities, as they help to promote independence, self-esteem, and a sense of accomplishment. Positive behaviors also help to build relationships, foster social skills, and improve overall quality of life.

Encourage individuals to take on tasks and responsibilities that promote independence, such as managing their own finances or preparing their own meals. Give individuals the opportunity to make choices and decisions that impact their own lives. This can include choosing their own activities or making decisions about their own. Provide positive reinforcement for individuals who engage in positive.

Allowing your person to take in active role in his/her own life unlock a more confident human being. It is the motivating factor to open up there world to try things they never thought they knew they could.

Chapter 5: Building Positive Relationships

Importance of Positive Relationships

Positive relationships play a critical role in the well-being and quality of life of individuals with developmental disabilities. Strong relationships can provide a sense of community and support, as well as offer opportunities for growth and learning. Positive relationships can also help to build self-esteem and increase overall happiness.

Some differently-abled people may seem void from emotions. It may be surprising to learn that is quite the opposite. They may feel and understand their feelings very deeply and have a hard time regulating how they feel and how they should respond to that feeling. The more they are offered a opportunity to see how others treat them or express their own range of emotion in a positive way around and with them, it can have huge impact on how their own responses are offered.

Strategies for Building Positive Relationships

Encourage individuals to develop effective communication skills, such as active listening and expressing emotions appropriately. These skills can help to foster positive relationships and prevent misunderstandings. This often requires active communication training. We are constantly talking and having exchanges throughout the day so why not encourage the same for your person. It's not as hard when you don't see them for their diagnosis rather for who they are as a person. It may seem like that would be a given. However, often this is something that happens subconsciously when routine care is rendered. Speak to your person and assume understanding. If your person responds alternatively that indicates a teachable moment. Don't flag the moment as it will make your person feel somehow. Telling them that they need to be corrected –doesn't help. Simply offer the adjust and move on.

Teach individuals how to navigate social situations and build positive relationships with others. This can include learning how to initiate conversations, make friends, and handle conflict in a healthy way. Being consistent with support in all situations especially helping other to learn what you know to smooth social interaction.

Most people have not had the amazing opportunity to meet your differently-abled individual. They may have only had access to acute situations that may or may not have given a good idea of what a person like your person really is like. It's the perfect time to teach them. This too should be effortless. Avoid putting your person on display, but serve as an example of how to interact and invite your person to join in. Explain to them what is happening before you begin from start to finish. If they do something that poses a challenge to this interaction, don't make a scene or make an excuse based on their diagnosis, simply help them to breathe or use their self- calming techniques and try again.

For all of these reasons refraining from being isolated is very important. Whereas some time allowed is necessary other time should be spent engaging in community activities. Encourage individuals to participate in community activities, such as volunteering or joining a recreational sports league. This can help to build relationships. The ability to thrive is reliant on adapting an acceptance attitude to go from " I don't belong here " to " it's okay to be myself here." Try to reach out to community members prior to visiting locations or events. Don't be afraid to talk about the challenges that exist and plan for a visit that can address your concerns beforehand. It can be a helpful practice to increase the amount of supportive events in your community. You can make the difference. Just speak up.

Chapter 6: Improving Engagement and Inclusion

Definition of Engagement and Inclusion

Engagement and inclusion refer to the active participation and involvement of individuals with developmental disabilities in their communities and daily life activities. This includes opportunities for meaningful relationships, employment, education, and recreation. They all are interrelated. Across your personal lifespan it is inevitable for you not to have discussions about each phase in great detail but it may be a series of revisiting topics as the person ages.

You may find that their interests and preferences change and so does their understanding of things around them. They may even return back to a certain phase closer to adulthood that you may have thought phased out when they were younger. This is natural but what poses the greatest challenge is shaping the awareness of the world around them to receive this ever changing or extremely consistent person.

Inclusion is about creating an environment where individuals are valued and accepted for who they are, and are provided with the support and resources they need to succeed. By promoting engagement and inclusion, individuals with autism can experience a greater sense of belonging, purpose, and fulfillment.

Techniques for Improving Engagement

It can be beneficial to offer community based vocational training opportunities that align with individuals' interests and abilities. This can help to improve engagement and provide a sense of purpose and fulfillment. Often volunteer roles may not have been thought of that may be perfect for your person–if only it existed. Why not create that opportunity and bring it to life. There is no harm in asking. A "no" can also positively open a discussion to why it doesn't exist and may even lead to future or alternate options that may ultimately support your person and others. This is a great way to have an impact in your community and strengthen the purpose for your person to exist in it.

There are countless ways to promote inclusive education opportunities that allow community members to learn alongside your differently-abled abled person. This can form a healthy relationship with people who differ from them. You've heard the old saying " Each one –teach one." This example at play help and can be a powerful tool to improve engagement and promote a sense of belonging.

This leads to your person having accessible transportation. Ensure that individuals have access to reliable and accessible options, allowing them to participate in community-based activities and access educational and employment opportunities. You can't expect them to do this on their own, but let me be honest, you may not travel everywhere they go but you can offer training to do activities such as calling a cab, and Uber, access a ride, following a bus schedule or scheduling a friend to transport to an activity.

Depending on your person's independence level, it may be worth a try to see how they respond to other means of travel outside of those offered solely by you. It might surprise you that they may need the space to learn new experiences. That's the benefit of having a supportive community. It's important for you to have trust in your community so that you can convey that say positive message to you differently-abled person.

A supportive community can greatly improve the engagement and inclusion by providing a safe and welcoming environment. Individuals can feel valued and accepted, and can actively participate in their communities. A supportive community can also provide opportunities for meaningful relationships, support, and growth.

Chapter 7: Building Self Esteem

Defining Self Esteem

Self-esteem refers to an individual's overall sense of self-worth and value. It is influenced by a range of factors, including relationships, experiences, and cultural values.

High self-esteem is associated with a range of positive outcomes, including improved mental health, greater resilience, and greater satisfaction with life. On the other hand, low self-esteem can have a negative impact on mental health and overall well-being. Here are some techniques for building self esteem

Encourage Positive Self-Talk: Teach individuals to engage in positive self-talk, focusing on their strengths and accomplishments rather than their weaknesses.

Provide Opportunities for Success: Offer individuals opportunities to experience success, such as through vocational training or educational programs.

Encourage Active Participation: Encourage individuals to take an active role in their own lives, making decisions and pursuing opportunities that align with their values and goals.

Promote Positive Relationships: Encourage individuals to build positive relationships with others, seeking out supportive and encouraging relationships that can help to boost self-esteem.

The Importance of Positive Reinforcement

Positive reinforcement is a powerful tool for building self-esteem. By recognizing and rewarding positive behaviors, individuals can feel valued and appreciated, leading to improved self-esteem and overall well-being.

It's important to provide specific and meaningful feedback to individuals, focusing on their strengths and accomplishments. This can help to reinforce positive behaviors and build a strong sense of self-worth and self-esteem. A reinforcement inventory is a healthy collection of things that are valuable to your person. It can be edible (food) , sensory (fidget toy), visual (looking at a show of interest), audio (favorite song) transitional (favorite place to go, running, or spinning). Keep in mind, where as these may be highly engaging and motivating from time to time, doing one thing too much can have a negative impact. It can be hard to move on to the next activity, leading to obsession or fixation with a particular interest.

Offering a range of things of interest for small increments can help your person, but hold onto one thing too long. Adding a timer can help the person know that it's time to move on and can take the fight out of transition with their scheduled day. You can also introduce what is called a visual list. Offer the times then remove from the list. Once time has passed, the item is collected or activity ends and the picture is removed. This signals to your person it is time to move on. This takes time to master, but I want to apply effectively to understand that there are other exciting things to look forward to that can develop.

Once this dynamic is understood you can introduce choice making and ask them to take part in creating their schedule. As the independence of your person grows. So should his or her ability to choose what and when things can become their interest and time offered to do as they may. This is no different from someone who doesn't have challenges. It is important to know the balance of offering support and empowering them to become more self-sufficient.

Chapter 8: Application of Supportive Techniques

To build self-esteem, it is recommended to use positive reinforcement techniques, such as praising and rewarding good behavior and accomplishments. It is also important to provide opportunities for young adults to succeed and experience a sense of accomplishment, through goal-setting activities and projects such as:

Sensory Integration:

Sensory integration refers to the process by which the brain processes and organizes sensory information from the environment. For young adults with autism or challenging cognitive development, sensory processing difficulties can impact their ability to engage in activities, form relationships, and complete tasks independently.

To support sensory integration, it is recommended to provide a sensory-friendly environment, with a variety of sensory experiences and opportunities for sensory regulation. It is also important to work with an occupational therapist to develop an individualized sensory diet that meets the unique needs of the young adult.

Communication:

Effective communication is a critical skill for young adults with autism or challenging cognitive development to be successful and independent in their daily lives. Some individuals may struggle with verbal communication, while others may have difficulty with social cues and nonverbal communication.

To improve communication skills, it is recommended to work with a speech therapist to develop an individualized communication plan. This may involve developing alternative forms of communication, such as sign language or a communication device, as well as working on social skills and conversation skills.

Giving Wait Time:

Giving wait time refers to allowing individuals the time they need to process a directive or request before expecting a response. For young adults with autism or challenging cognitive development, wait time can be especially important, as they may need extra time to process information and respond appropriately.

When working with young adults with autism or challenging cognitive development, it is recommended to give wait time and avoid rushing or pushing for an immediate response. This can help to reduce stress and anxiety, and promote a sense of control and independence.

Implementing the strategies and techniques discussed offers an opportunity for parents and caregivers to empower young adults with autism or challenging cognitive development to become more independent, engaged, and included in their communities. By focusing on developing essential life skills, such as independent work skills, self-advocacy, self-determination, positive behaviors, engagement and inclusion, self-esteem, and supporting sensory integration, communication, and wait time, young adults can reach their full potential and lead fulfilling lives.

Chapter 9: Ways to Get Started

Here are 10 ways to support your person in developing and applying skills for life:

Money Management: Teach your young adults how to handle money by assigning tasks such as paying bills, making change, and creating a budget. Don't just do it for them. Start with one step such as giving them a dollar to exchange then move to counting, adding and storing money on their person.

Cooking: Assign a night that your young adult can participate in serving a meal. They should also be included in meal planning, grocery shopping, and preparing meals. This will not only improve their cooking skills but also help develop food safety knowledge and nutrition.

Cleaning: Assign tasks such as cleaning the kitchen, bathroom, or laundry room to help develop household management skills. There is someone everyone can do including setting and clearing the table, taking out the trash, sorting recyclables, helping with the dishwasher or laundry. The possibilities are endless. You might even learn that some of these activities are enjoyable for your person.

Personal Care: Teach young adults how to maintain personal hygiene and grooming by assigning tasks such as bathing, brushing teeth, and getting dressed. This can be very helpful to identify areas of improvement, sensory challenges and even medical needs. Sometimes concerns such as frequent urination can lead to discussion of diet and exercise, the need for special toiletries and adaptive tools, types of clothing or medication needed. Knowing these points of clarity can help alleviate problems in other areas that can improve your person's well-being.

Technology: Encourage the use of technology by assigning tasks such as typing a document, sending an email, and using a calculator. Assistive devices, Augmentative Communication devices, or other advancement can be expensive but you may find if you research your resources there are insurance and grant opportunities to support this addition.

Communication Skills: Often, differently- abled people have a limited amount of communicators to practice with. Every opportunity is a chance to practice . Be mindful to introduce new people to communicate with so increase their chances of meeting and speaking to different people.

Problem Solving: Encourage your person to work through problems on their own by assigning tasks such as troubleshooting a technical issue, or finding a solution to a difficult real-time scenario. Don't just figure it out or do the work for them. They need opportunities to practice– especially without us.

Time Management: Teach them to manage their time effectively by assigning tasks such as setting a schedule for the day and completing tasks within a certain timeframe. Using timers, counters and count down will make expectations clear and limit confusion.

Organizational Skills: Support the development of organizational skills by assigning tasks such as sorting and filing documents, and keeping a tidy workspace. If you pick up after them you are sending the implied message that no matter what you and those around them will always do it for them. Let go and let them become more accountable for their actions.

Environmental Awareness: Encourage awareness of their surroundings by assigning tasks such as sorting recyclables, composting, and conserving energy. This will help them become more engaged with the world they are actively living in.

Chapter 10: Community Inclusion

Here are some tips to promoting community inclusion:

Community volunteer work and Employment Opportunities: Encouraging community volunteer work can help them feel valued and connected to their community. No job is too small. Find ways to be apart even if it's an annual community event.

Social clubs and groups: Joining social clubs or groups that align with the individual's interests can help them build relationships and social skills.

Recreational activities: Participation in recreational activities such as sports, dance classes, or art classes can help them develop new skills. Birthday parties can be a challenge but if there's an event that your person enjoy why not inform the director to make it an open party plan that is informally a birthday celebration with or without the fixing. Some scenarios can lead to sensory overload and that is a point of consideration for your person ,but you can be creative on how this can be organized.

Community events: Attending community events such as festivals, concerts, and parades can help individuals with autism experience new environments and activities. If they don't yet exist, request they become a part. It may be just that no one has asked. You may be the one to do it.

Library events: Encouraging differently-abled individuals to attend library events such as book clubs, author readings, and workshops can help them connect with others and develop new interests. Seeing someone with challenges such as their can impact their determination as it builds the connection for how they see themselves apart of society

Community classes: Encouraging individuals with autism to take community classes such as cooking, woodworking, or computer skills can help them develop new skills and interests. Always promote trying new things.

Religious or spiritual groups: Joining religious or spiritual groups can help individuals with autism connect with others and feel a sense of belonging.

Service projects: Whenever possible help them to participate in service projects such as cleaning up parks or volunteering at a local food bank can help them make a positive impact on their community. It may require some preparation but the results might be worth it. A sense of accomplishment or a winning smile can make the planning phase worth its weight in gold.

Ways to Advocate for Community Support

Education and Awareness

Educate family, teachers, and community members about autism and its impact on individuals itself. This will help them better understand and support their needs. Open communication between all stakeholders involved in the individual's life. This includes sharing information about their needs, goals, and challenges. Collaboration between family, teachers, and community members to ensure that everyone is working together to support the individual's growth and development.
If you do say anything, no one knows. Don't be afraid to speak up. Advocate for the individual's rights and needs in various settings, including school, community, and workplace.

Often it is necessary to demonstrate to family, teachers, and community members how to use positive reinforcement to support desired behaviors and reduce challenging behaviors. Let it be a general practice for all those who impact their lives. As they grow, they change and so should the strategies that support them. You may have to change technique or build on them but expecting what used to work to remain consistent is not a healthy way to approach the changes needed to keep up with your differently-abled person. Equip yourself with all the tools you need to be successful.

Stay in constant communication and note updates with varied family members , different teachers, and frequently sought out community members to actively offer various activities and events, promoting a sense of belonging, community and the importance of change. Change can be scary as well but absolutely necessary for growth. This doesn't just apply to the differently-abled person but those who support them as well. You can unknowingly hinder their growth if you fear necessary changes.

Advocate for accommodations that support the individual's needs and abilities, such as sensory breaks, extra support, and adapted materials. If it does exist, create it. If you don't know how to ask. There are many YouTube tutorials, workshops and other parents or caretakers that won't hesitate to share. Having a friend who had similar experiences can help boost your willingness to try new approaches to problem solving that can then be taught to your person.

Request family support and uphold the individual's independence, by gradually increasing responsibilities and promoting self-help skills. Remember to be flexible, give time for them to get used to something new as none of us are perfect and help them become adaptable in their approach to do more and more on their own. As they become comfortable, ensure that they become involved in decision-making and problem-solving situations to put it in active practice. This will promote a sense of self-determination and control over their lives.

Assistive and Augmentative Communication

We have reference technology earlier but let's take a closer look at it. Assistive and Augmentative Communication(AAC) devices can an essential tool for individuals with autism or challenging cognitive development to improve their functional communication skills and increase their independence. These devices help individuals with limited speech or communication skills to express their needs, wants, and emotions effectively. In a vocational setting, AAC devices can play a critical role in unlocking the potential of individuals with autism and supporting them in performing various tasks.

For example, an individual with autism who works in a retail store can use an AAC device to communicate with customers, coworkers, and supervisors. The device can be programmed with common phrases, questions, and responses to help the individual interact effectively and efficiently in the workplace. In a vocational task, an individual can use an AAC device to communicate their progress, ask for assistance, or provide feedback to their supervisor.

In an art, business, technology or agriculture setting, an individual with autism can use an AAC device to communicate their ideas, ask for clarification, and collaborate with others. These devices can also help individuals with autism to better understand instructions, follow step-by-step procedures, and complete tasks independently.

Unlocking the power of AAC devices in vocational settings can significantly improve the functional communication skills and independence by providing them with the tools they need to communicate effectively, so they can be more successful and contribute to the community in meaningful ways. It is important for educators, parents, and care providers to understand the benefits of AAC devices and to provide individuals with autism with the support they need to use these devices effectively.

ABOUT THE AUTHOR

As a parent of a 21 year daughter with autism, I understand the difficulties and challenges of navigating the education system for individuals with autism. My journey as a parent has equipped me with first-hand knowledge of the lack of services available to support autistic adults, limited funding to support parents or educators, and a lack of awareness in the work environment to provide meaningful opportunities for individuals with autism to work in their own community.

The journey has not been easy, with limited help and the constant judgment of others. I have had to make sacrifices such as excusing myself from public events or having community members call the police because they didn't know how to support my daughter– when all she was trying to do was communicate and they had no clue of what that looked like. When I realized that these were the teachable moments I should celebrate, I started to empower myself differently and spoke out in an effort to impact change – right when it was happening. Sure it can be scary and extremely frustrating but what an example to work with in itself. I constantly chose to demonstrate the self- control I want my daughter to have and self-advocacy I wish for my daughter to demonstrate.

 Ultimately finding her own voice. I also learned the importance of setting up the right environment, from the type of clothing she wears, the food she eats, the activities she is involved in, the car I drive, and the preparation for traveling. Going the distance to reduce triggers that may lead to behavioral outbursts has helped to improve the way we communicate with each other. I have learned that behaviors are a form of communication and I just had to listen. Of course there is a difference from her shaping my behaviors to get her way but again these are teachable moments– for both of us to learn how to better communicate. I offer her real responses, yes, even the no's have a way of helping your differently abled person to grow and adapt. As ready as I remain for those setbacks, I am just as eager to create opportunities to try new things on her own.

This is why I am so passionate about equipping others with the knowledge in this book. No. It won't fix all of the problems you have ,but it will help sharpen your outlook. By understanding the complexities of autism and the challenges that individuals with autism face, we can create a more inclusive and supportive community– for us all. By educating ourselves, we can provide meaningful opportunities for individuals with autism to live, learn and work in their own communities. This book is a tool to help bring awareness and understanding to the autism community and to provide parents, educators, and communities with the resources they need to support individuals with autism in their journey.

I can't say enough how much I understand the struggles and challenges that come with navigating the journey of supporting them. One of the biggest lessons I have learned is the importance of knowing when to ask for help. With limited resources and support staff in the community, it can often feel like you're on your own and drowning, but that doesn't have to be the case.

The transition into adulthood can be a difficult and overwhelming process for individuals with autism, but it doesn't have to be. By equipping yourself with the knowledge and resources available, you can ensure that your loved one has a successful and fulfilling life. The goal should be to create a positive and supportive environment that promotes self-esteem, independence, and overall happiness.

It's important to remember that letting go and seeking help is not a guilt-free decision. Society often places a negative stigma on individuals with autism, but it's important to ignore those harmful beliefs and focus on the well-being of your loved one. The right support and resources can make all the difference in their lives and can lead to increased independence and happiness.

I get it! The struggle is way too real when navigating the journey but it's important not to allow you emotions to silence your actions. Don't hide away and feel sorry for yourself or limit how far your love one can thrive – just because the world hasn't expressed readiness to receive your message. It's also important to know when to ask for help and seek out alternative resources, such as trusted group homes, alternative family living, treatment apartment programs, and independent care facilities.

Whereas the transition into adulthood can be difficult, but with the right support and resources your community and how you navigate can have a huge impact on what you and your person gets out of it. With these inclusive strategies, you can create a future that can be a successful and fulfilling process. It is a choice you and your person have to bring yourselves to make.

 Let's work towards creating a more inclusive and supportive environment for individuals with autism. Chances are it won't be done for you and yes their is lots of work to do. It's about time we encourage the ones we love to find and use their voice to unapologetically celebrate being differently abled. Remember, the journey is ongoing, but with the right tools and support, it can be a fulfilling role to find yourself in and an "AU-Some" world to live in for both you and I !

-AU&I

Made in the USA
Columbia, SC
21 February 2023